Life Lessons

Life Lessons

Skooler Books

ISBN : 978-93-340-4920-6

Dedicated to
MY DAD

With mighty wings, the Eagle soars,

Teaching the young, to aim for more.

With every risk, dreams take flight,

So be bold, and reach new heights.

Rooster's lesson, simple and wise,
Early to bed, early to rise.

With rested minds and eager eyes,
Embrace the day with joyful cries.

So rise up early, don't delay,
Embrace the morning, seize the day.

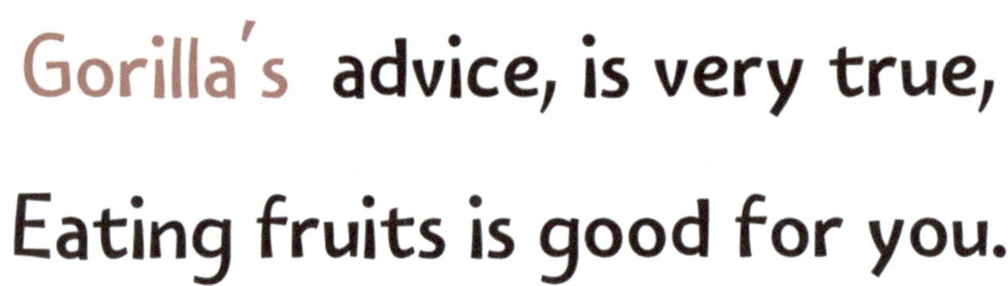

Gorilla's advice, is very true,
Eating fruits is good for you.

With every bite, feel your best,
Healthy choices pass his test.

Turtle mom with gentle eyes,

Gives a wise and sound advice.

Life is journey , and not a race

so enjoy it fully, in your pace

Love the journey, and be on grind

Perfection comes, just give it time.

In the jungle, a Parrot springs,

With his young, under the wings.

"Be on time," she sings with cheer,

And never be late, is her lesson so clear.

The chubby Bear, has a secret to share,

"Sleep for eight hours," he says with care.

Sleeping right, our bodies mend,

To face the day, strength it lends.

So close your eyes, let worries depart,

In a peaceful sleep, we nourish the heart.

Dolphin mom in the ocean blue,

gives her young an important clue.

With daily practice, you hone your arts,

And chance of failure, further departs.

Peacock speaks with gentle eyes,
For his young, to not to lie.

Speaking truth is always right,
In every choice, in every sight.

In her words, a moral is seen,
That, honesty is the best routine.

In the yard, with hurdles in sight,

Dog leaps over, with all his might.

With every jump, he shows the way,

To face challenges, come what may.

.

Mommy Sheep is fluffy and white,

Teaches young ones, to be polite.

To ask for something, say 'please', not seize,

And follow with 'thank you', like a breeze.

Beside her lamb, with feet so neat,

Her lessons in kindness, oh so sweet.

Mommy Squirrel is soft and sweet,
Gathering nuts with her nimble feet.

Saving is vital, a lesson she shared,
To be ready for unknown, and be prepared.

Cheetah mom is running wild,

Racing her cub, side by side.

"Run each day," she purrs with joy,

Exercise is good, what she employs.

Through grassy plains, as they flee,

A lesson on fitness, is set free.

Cunning Fox is eager to teach,

To embrace curiosity, is her speech.

In Life's every unseen part,

Wonders await for the curious heart.

On a wooden log, a green Snake lies,

Imparts the truth, with no disguise.

Your looks may differ, in shape and size,

But despite the odds, you can rise.

In her words, a lesson so wise,

"Embrace your flaws," is the advice.

Hippo mom, with a purple skin,

Teaches her young, how to swim.

"Balance your tasks," she implores,

Find harmony, and unlock new doors.

In his kingdom, Lion roams free,

Teaches a lesson, come and see.

With a mighty roar, he shows the way,

To be positive, come what may.

So heed his roar, and listen close,

Fill your heart with good vibes dose.

In the garden, under the sky,
Baby Rabbit gives veggies a try.

With crunchy bite, Mommy shares,
Eating greens keeps you strong and fair.

In the desert, where sand is dry,

Camel teaches, with a knowing eye.

"Drink lots of water," his sage advice,

"To stay hydrated," to be precise.

By the river, an Elephant glows,

Teaches her young , gentle and slow.

"Bath daily, my love," she says with pride,

In the waters, your worries subside.

Life's lesson, in their playful bath,

Daily cleansing, is the right path.

Please leave a Review

Dr. H T

9 789334 049206